Let's Read and Write
... that's it!

AF203323

Workbook 4

Susanne McCafferty
Tina Kresse

illustriert von
Elisabeth Lottermoser

Bestell-Nr. 1902-35 · ISBN 978-3-619-19235-9

© 2011 Mildenberger Verlag GmbH, 77610 Offenburg
www.mildenberger-verlag.de
E-Mail: info@mildenberger-verlag.de

Auflage   7   6   5   4
Jahr   2022   2021   2020   2019

Das Werk und seine Teile sind urheberrechtlich geschützt. Jede Nutzung in anderen als den gesetzlich zugelassenen Fällen bedarf der vorherigen schriftlichen Einwilligung des Verlages. Hinweis zu § 52 a UrhG: Weder das Werk noch seine Teile dürfen ohne eine solche Einwilligung eingescannt und in ein Netzwerk eingestellt werden. Dies gilt auch für Intranets von Schulen und sonstigen Bildungseinrichtungen.

Bezugsmöglichkeiten
Alle Titel des Mildenberger Verlags erhalten Sie unter: www.mildenberger-verlag.de oder im Buchhandel. Jede Buchhandlung kann alle Titel direkt über den Mildenberger Verlag beziehen. Ausnahmen kann es bei Titeln mit Lösungen geben: Hinweise hierzu finden Sie in unserem aktuellen Gesamtprogramm.

Bildquellenverzeichnis
Alle Fotos: © Fotolia.de bis auf folgende Ausnahmen:
„British coins (tail side)", „British coins (head side)", „Bagpiper": © Susanne McCafferty/Tina Kresse;
„Celtic Park football stadium": © Celtic F.C. Limited. Used with kind permission; „underground station": wikimedia.de

Redaktion: Tobias Pfaff
Grafik: Mildenberger Verlag GmbH

Druck: AZ Druck und Datentechnik GmbH, 87437 Kempten
Gedruckt auf umweltfreundlichen Papieren

Topics

Welcome Back

Can you remember Anna and
Michael? Of course you can.
But we think you can remember
many more things from last year.
In this page you see two
mindmaps. Do you think you can
fill in some words? Your teacher will help you.
Or you take your 3rd class workbook or your portfolio folder.

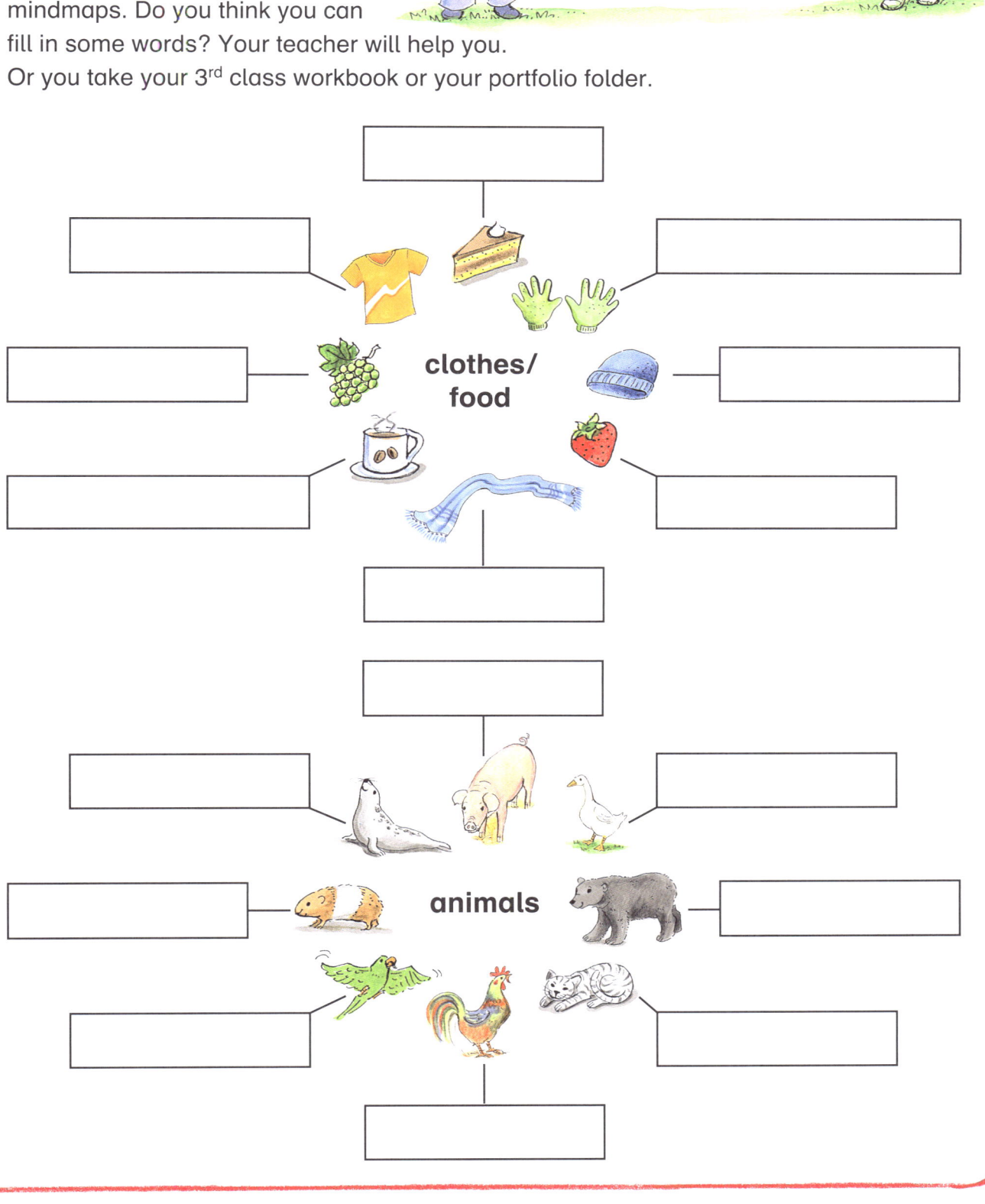

clothes/
food

animals

Welcome to the British Isles

1. Can you remember the countries and capital cities on this map?
   Write the correct words in CAPITAL letters.

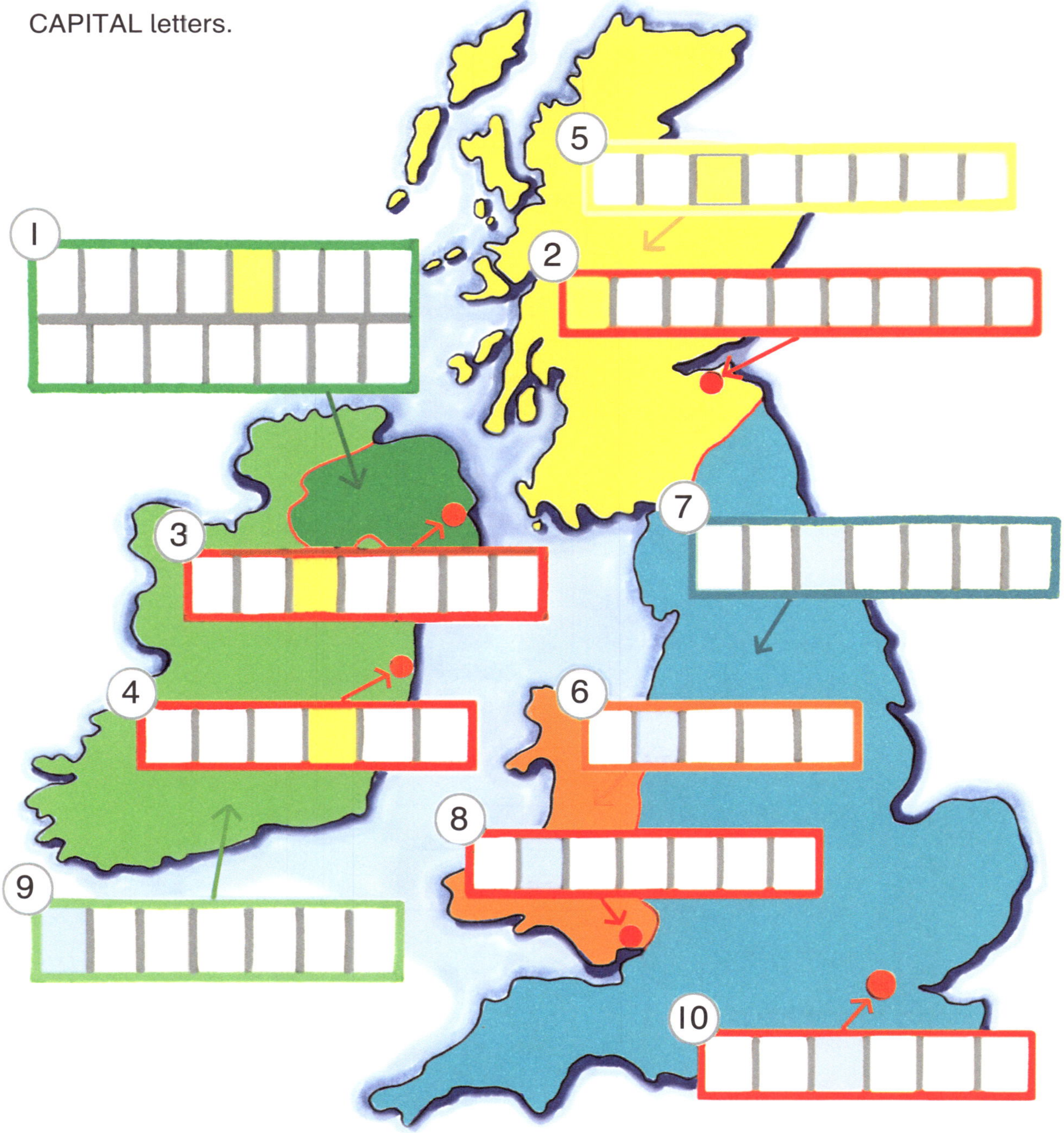

Countries: England, Wales, Ireland, Northern Ireland, Scotland
Capitals: Dublin, Edinburgh, Cardiff, Belfast, London

2. Write the marked letter above the numbers.

1	2	3	4	5	6	7	8	9	10

The Children in the Workbook

Hello _____ (Fill in your name!)

These are the children in the workbook:

Anna and Michael are brother and sister and come from Edinburgh in Scotland. Anna is nine years old, Michael is ten. Anna is wearing a green and white and red and yellow T-shirt, Michael is wearing an orange T-shirt.

Sheila comes from Belfast in Northern Ireland. She is 9 years old. She has long red hair and blue eyes.

Lisa and Peter are brother and sister, too and come from Stuttgart in Germany. Lisa is ten years old, Peter is nine. Lisa has short blond hair and Peter is wearing a Germany T-shirt.

Ian comes from Dublin in Ireland. He is ten years old. On his blue shirt there is a green shamrock.

Diana comes from Cardiff in Wales. She is nine years old. She has got a red toy dragon.

David comes from London in England. He is nine years old, too. He is wearing a London T-shirt.

1. This is what they look like. Please find out who is who and write the names under the pictures.

Welcome to the British Isles

1. Do you know the flags? Write the name of the country under the right flag.

_____ _____ _____ _____ _____

2. Can you fill in the missing words and sentences?

Hello David!
Where are you from?
I'm from London.
David is from England.

Hello Sheila!
Where are you from?
I'm from Belfast.
Sheila is from

_____ .

Hello Diana! Where are you from?

_____ Cardiff. Diana _____ .

Hello Anna!
Where are you from?

_____ Edinburgh.

_____ .

Hello Ian!

_____

_____ Dublin. _____ .

And you? Where are you from? _____

Where Do They Live?

12, London Road, Cardiff

4, Richmond Drive, Edinburgh

35/2, Holland Road, London

28, Country Lane, Dublin

7, South Street, Belfast

1. Where do they live?

David: I live in a big house. In the house there is not only my family, but other

families, too. I live in _____

Diana: I live in a nice house. It has only one floor. The car is in front of the house.

I live in _____

Ian: I live in a house made of wood. It is made from many trees. And it is brown.

I live in _____

Sheila: I live in a semi-detached house. There are two families in the house. It has

got two front doors. I live in _____

Anna: I live in a cottage. This is a little house with a garden in the countryside of

Scotland. I live in _____

2. And you? Where do you live?

I live in _____ , _____ , _____

3. And your friend? Where does he or she live?

_____ , _____ , _____

At Home

1. This is Anna's and Michael's house. What can you see?

2. Can you find the 15 parts of the house in the quiz?

g	s	i	t	t	i	n	g	r	o	o	m	a	b	e	d	r	o	o	m
a	b	a	t	h	r	o	o	m	x	k	i	t	c	h	e	n	q	r	t
r	d	i	n	i	n	g	r	o	o	m	w	t	y	a	r	t	x	o	o
d	c	v	o	n	m	g	a	r	a	g	e	i	p	l	o	i	u	o	i
e	x	y	a	s	d	f	g	h	j	k	l	c	e	l	l	a	r	f	l
n	q	c	h	i	m	n	e	y	w	s	t	u	d	y	n	p	o	m	e
c	h	i	l	d	r	e	n	s	b	e	d	r	o	o	m	e	r	t	t

In the Flat

1. There are many pieces of furniture.
   Connect the pictures to the words.

radio

washbasin

toilet

armchair

lamp

cupboard

shower

bed

table

chair

couch

desk

plant

tv-set

door

2. How many of all these things can you find in the house on page 8?

   There are _____

   _____

   _____

   _____

3. Which pieces of furniture are in your home?

   At home we have got _____

   _____

   _____

In the Flat

sitting room

kitchen

1. What can you see in the sitting room? Circle ◯ the things in the picture!

   There is a couch in the sitting room.

   There is _____

   _____

   _____

   _____

2. What can you see in the kitchen? Circle ◯ the things in the picture!

   There is a table in the kitchen.

   There is _____

   _____

   _____

   _____

Where Are They?

children's bedroom

bathroom

1. What can you see in the children's room?
   Circle ⭕ the things in the picture!
   There is a bed in the children's room.

   There is _____

   _____

   _____

   _____

2. What can you see in the bathroom?
   Circle ⭕ the things in the picture! There is a shower in the bathroom.

   There is _____

   _____

   _____

   _____

In the Flat

A Game

pencil   toothpaste   tv-set   soap   carpet   mug   cup   washing mashine   cooker   spoon   knife   fork

Left side (top to bottom): plates · towel · desk · fridge · glass · face cloth · pot · lamp · pear · wash basin · cd-player · chair · bottle

Right side (top to bottom): plant · curtains · cupboard · shampoo · apple · shower · computer · armchair · table · bed · bookshelf

Bottom: tea · coffee · sandwich · scissors · milk · sugar · dish cloth · dish towel · cookie · tooth brush · chimney

Play with a friend. Take a coloured pencil and a game piece each. Put the two game pieces on the "start"-square. Your friend tells you where you have got to go (go left … steps, go right … steps, go to the top … steps, go to the bottom … steps). If you can name the thing in that square you may colour the square. If you can't, you may not colour it. If you reach an empty square you can colour it straight away. Then it's your friend's turn. The winner is the one who coloured most squares. If you like you can play again in your friend's workbook.

What Do You Do in the House?

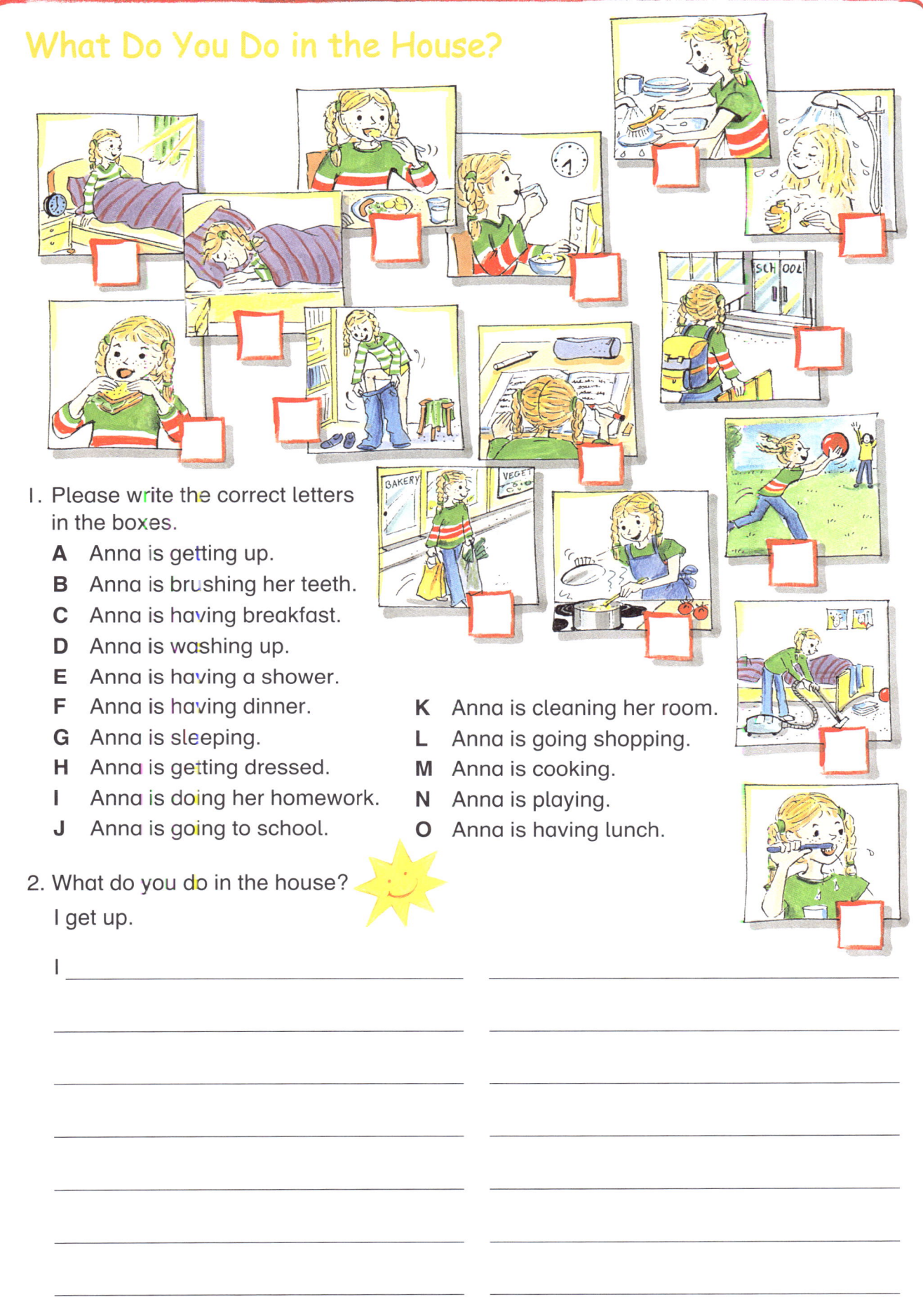

1. Please write the correct letters
   in the boxes.

   A   Anna is getting up.

   B   Anna is brushing her teeth.

   C   Anna is having breakfast.

   D   Anna is washing up.

   E   Anna is having a shower.

   F   Anna is having dinner.

   G   Anna is sleeping.

   H   Anna is getting dressed.

   I   Anna is doing her homework.

   J   Anna is going to school.

   K   Anna is cleaning her room.

   L   Anna is going shopping.

   M   Anna is cooking.

   N   Anna is playing.

   O   Anna is having lunch.

2. What do you do in the house?

   I get up.

   I _____

In the Flat

1. Can you name the 15 things you do during the day?

x	h	a	v	e	b	r	e	a	k	f	a	s	t	x	x
x	c	w	x	x	x	x	x	x	x	g	e	t	u	p	s
p	l	a	y	x	d	o	h	o	m	e	w	o	r	k	l
x	e	s	x	x	b	r	u	s	h	t	e	e	t	h	e
x	a	h	x	x	x	x	x	x	d	x	x	x	x	x	e
x	n	u	x	c	x	x	x	x	r	x	x	x	x	x	p
x	x	p	x	o	x	x	h	a	v	e	l	u	n	c	h
g	o	s	h	o	p	p	i	n	g	s	x	x	x	x	x
x	x	x	k	x	g	o	t	o	s	c	h	o	o	l
x	h	a	v	e	a	s	h	o	w	e	r	x	x	x	x
x	x	x	x	x	x	h	a	v	e	d	i	n	n	e	r

2. What do you do at this time?

 I get up at half past six.

 _____ at half past seven.

 _____ at half past two.

 _____ at half past four.

 _____ at half past six.

 _____ at quarter past twelve.

3. Play pantomime and ask your friend: What am I doing?

Portfolio: Welcome Back - At Home

I know the countries in the British Isles.
In the British Isles there are five countries:

_____

_____

I know the capitals of three of these countries.
The capital of England is _____

_____

_____

I can write down my address.

I live in _____

I can write down in English what is in the house:

_____

_____

That was :)   :| :(

Portfolio: Welcome Back - At Home

Ich kann schon auf Englisch verstehen:

welche Länder zu den Britischen Inseln gehören	☺ 😐 ☹
wenn jemand von den Hauptstädten der Britischen Inseln erzählt	☺ 😐 ☹
wenn mir jemand auf Englisch sagt, wo er wohnt	☺ 😐 ☹
wenn jemand von den Zimmern im Haus erzählt	☺ 😐 ☹
wenn jemand von Möbeln im Haus erzählt	☺ 😐 ☹
wo etwas ist oder wo ich hingehen soll	☺ 😐 ☹
was jemand im Haus tut	☺ 😐 ☹

Ich kann schon auf Englisch sagen:

welche Länder zu den Britischen Inseln gehören	☺ 😐 ☹
welche Hauptstädte zu den Ländern gehören	☺ 😐 ☹
wo ich wohne (mit genauer Adressenangabe auf Englisch)	☺ 😐 ☹
wie die Zimmer im Haus heißen	☺ 😐 ☹
wie die Möbel heißen	☺ 😐 ☹
wo etwas im Haus ist oder wo jemand hingehen soll	☺ 😐 ☹
was jemand im Haus tut und was ich tue	☺ 😐 ☹

Ich kann schon auf Englisch fragen:

wo jemand wohnt	☺ 😐 ☹
wo etwas im Haus ist	☺ 😐 ☹
was jemand im Haus tut	☺ 😐 ☹

Ich kann schon auf Englisch lesen:

die Namen der Länder auf den Britischen Inseln und die Hauptstädte	☺ 😐 ☹
eine englische Adresse	☺ 😐 ☹
die Namen der Räume im Haus	☺ 😐 ☹
die Namen der Möbelstücke	☺ 😐 ☹
was jemand im Haus tut	☺ 😐 ☹

 Ich bin mit mir sehr zufrieden. ◯

 Ich finde, es war schon ganz gut. ◯

 Ich hoffe, das wird noch besser. ◯

Christmas

In Britain children write a wishlist to Santa Claus.

1. Here you can write your own wishlist:

> Dear Santa,
> for Christmas I want
>
> _____
>
> _____

2. Can you fill in the missing words?

Santa Got Stuck up the Chimney

It was _ _ _ _ _ _ _ _ _ _ _ _ _ _ _. Anna and Michael prepared everything for

Santa. They put a glass of _ _ _ _ and a plate of _ _ _ _ _ _ _ onto the

little table in the _ _ _ _ _ _ _ _ _ _ _ _ _. The _ _ _ _ _ _ _ _ _ _ _ hung

over the fireplace. The _ _ _ _ _ _ _ _ _ _ _ _ _ _ _ was decorated with

lights and _ _ _ _ _ _ _ _ _ _ _ _ _ _ _ _ _ _ _. They put out the fire

and went to bed. At night Santa came through the _ _ _ _ _ _ _ _. He saw the

cookies and the milk. Every time when he put a _ _ _ _ _ _ _ _ under the tree

or in a stocking he took a cookie and a sip of milk. Then he was tired and sat in the

_ _ _ _ _ _ _ _ _ . But the armchair broke. He took his sack, went to the

_ _ _ _ _ _ _ _ _ _ and climbed up the chimney. Ooops, he could not get further.

He was too _ _ _. In the morning Anna and Michael saw _ _ _ _ _ stuck up the

chimney. They pulled him out. He ran out of the door and shouted:

" _ _ _ _ _ _ _ _ _ _ _ _ _ _ _ !" And away he flew in his _ _ _ _ _ _ _

with the _ _ _ _ _ _ _ _. But nobody believed Anna and Michael.

> present   sleigh   cookies   sitting room   Christmas tree   reindeer
> Christmas tree balls   Christmas Eve   chimney   armchair   milk
> fireplace   fat   Santa   stockings   Merry Christmas

Christmas

1. Can you find the Christmas words?
   If you can find them all you will get a solution sentence!

2. We wish you a _____

In the Course of the Year

1. Can you fill in the missing words?

The Seasons

_____ is the first season of the year.

It's cold and frosty and _____ is here.

In spring the first _____ start to grow,

the sun shines _____ and melts the snow.

In _____ the children are happy and have fun,

they can swim – it's nice and _____ in the sun.

Autumn brings _____ and lots of rain,

the leaves change colour – it's getting _____ again.

What are they called – the _____ of the year?

I think you know it – there are clever children in here!

cold   snow   warmer   summer   Winter   wind   seasons   flowers   hot

The seasons are called _____

2. Can you answer these questions in full sentences?

What is the first season of the year?

_____

What happens in spring?

_____

What can children do in summer?

_____

What does autumn do?

_____

What is the weather like in winter?

_____

The Months

1. Which month is it?

In Germany we celebrate carnival. _____

Christmas is celebrated. _____

Spring starts. _____

Autumn starts. _____

We can go on holiday. _____

Easter bunny comes. _____

We can go skiing. _____

It is very windy and we can fly kites. _____

2. There are some months missing. Can you write them down?

_____

3. Write down the months you like and what you wear in these months.

swimming costume   jacket   T-shirt   snow boots   pullover   rain hat

wolly hat   wellies   baseball cap   scarf   sandals   trunks   gloves

I like January and I wear snow boots, jacket, gloves, scarf, woolly hat and pullover.

_____

_____

_____

In the Course of the Year

1. This is Anna's and Michael's timetable. But the days are missing. Can you fill them in?

TIMETABLE

Time	Monday				
8.30 – 8.50	Assembly				
8.50 – 9.50	English	Science	English	English	Maths
9.50 – 10.50	Maths	English	Art	English	Maths
10.50 – 11.10	Break				
11.10 – 12.10	R.E.	Maths	Maths	P.E.	Computer
12.10 – 12.55	Lunch Break				
1.00 – 2.00	Geography	Drama	Science	Maths	Music
2.00 – 3.00	P.E.	Drama	Science	Art	English

2. Some of the subjects we do not know in Germany.

   Please fill in your timetable: Please try and use the English words:

TIMETABLE

Time				

What Do You Do Every Day?

I. What can you do in your free time? Connect the words to the pictures.

go swimming

ride a horse

go climbing

ride a bike

read books

play football

go bowling

play volleyball

play an instrument

play games

go jogging

play computer games

do homework

meet friends

go to the playground

go dancing

What Do You Do Every Day?

1. Read about Sheila's week.

   I'm Sheila from Belfast. On Monday in the afternoon I ride a horse. I am a big horse fan. On Tuesday I go swimming. On Wednesday I meet my friends, because school finishes early. On Thursday I ride my bike or play games. On Friday I play volleyball. On Saturday I go dancing. I do Irish Dancing. On Sunday I go bowling – I love that! Oh – and of course – every day I do my homework. What about you?

2. Sheila says:

   "On Monday I ride a horse.

   On Tuesday _____

   _____

   On _____

   _____

   On _____

   _____

   On _____

   _____

   On _____

   _____

   On _____

   _____ "

   What do **you** do that day?

   On Monday I _____

   On Tuesday _____

   _____

   On _____

   _____

   On _____

   _____

   On _____

   _____

   On _____

   _____

   On _____

   _____

3. Which is your favourite day of the week? Why?

   My favourite day is _____ , because

   _____

   > I can do my favourite hobby, I don't have to go to school, I meet friends, I can do things with my family …

What Do You Eat During the Day?

1. There are many meals. Can you connect the pictures to the correct names?

British breakfast   bread, butter and jam

nothing   cereals

biscuits   pizza

cake   pasta

pancakes   sandwich

vegetables   salad

2. There are five meals during the day. Please fill in the missing time of the day and the food you like for this meal.

> **at night, in the afternoon, in the morning, in the evening, at lunchtime**

_____ I have breakfast. For breakfast I eat _____

_____

_____ I have lunch. For lunch I like _____

_____

_____ I have tea. For tea I like _____

_____

_____ I have dinner. For dinner I like _____

_____

_____ I do not eat. I sleep.

The Time

1. What's the time?

  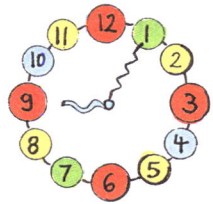

 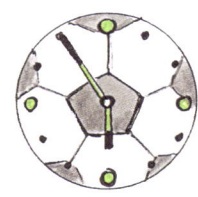 

To remind you:

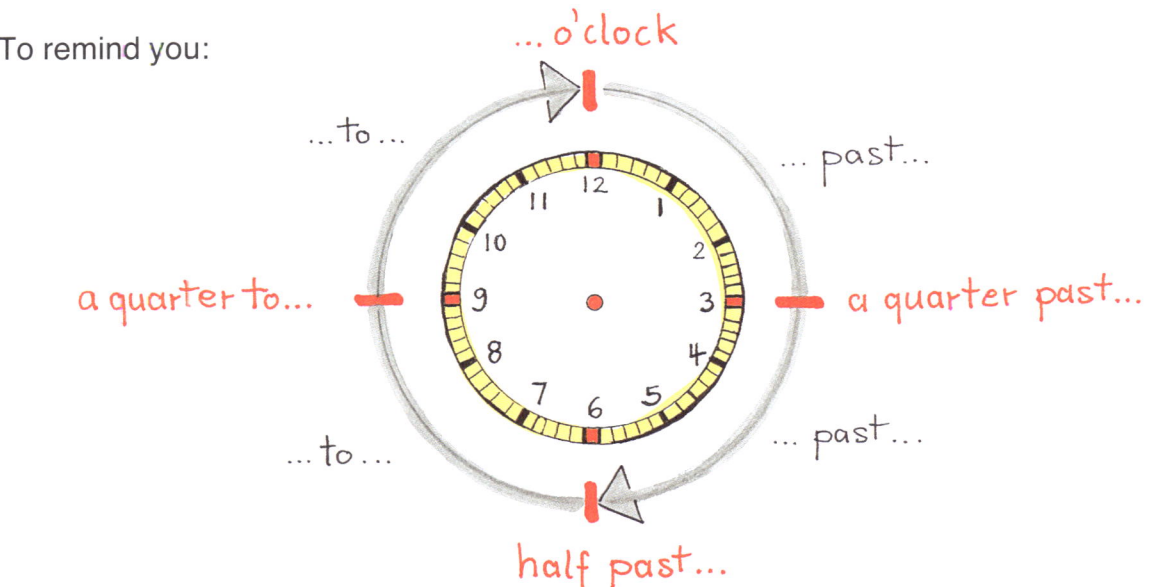

Today

1. Write the dates for today.

Month

January   February
March   April
May   June   July
August   September
October   November
December

Date

'st   'nd   'rd   'th

1st   2nd

4th   7th

21st   23rd

Year

2018   2021   2017

2020   2016

2015   2024   2022

2019   2023

Day of the week

Monday   Tuesday
Wednesday
Thursday   Sunday
Friday
Saturday

Weather

warm

cold   hot

cool

Season

winter

spring

summer

autumn

Time

Draw the clock hands and write the time:

_____

2. Please answer these questions about today in full sentences.

What day is today? _____

What date is today? _____

What is the weather like? _____

What season is today? _____

What is the time? _____

Portfolio: In the Course of the Year

I know the seasons.
What are they called?

_____

I know the days of the week.
What are they called?

_____

_____

I know the months.
Write the names:

_____

_____

I know the date.

Today is: _____

I know the time.
Draw the clock hands and write the time:

_____

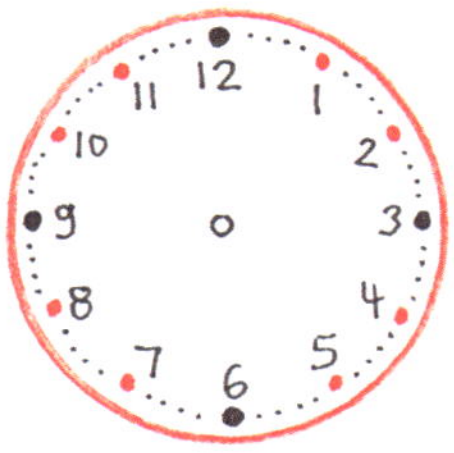

That was 😊 😐 ☹

Portfolio: In the Course of the Year

Ich kann schon auf Englisch verstehen:

wenn über Kalender und Zeit gesprochen wird	😊 😐 ☹️
wenn jemand nach der Zeit fragt	😊 😐 ☹️
wenn jemand das Datum sagt	😊 😐 ☹️
die Tageszeit und die Mahlzeit, die dazu gehört	😊 😐 ☹️

Ich kann schon auf Englisch sagen:

welcher Monat im Moment ist	😊 😐 ☹️
welcher Wochentag heute ist	😊 😐 ☹️
wie spät es ist	😊 😐 ☹️
das heutige Datum	😊 😐 ☹️
die Tageszeit und die dazugehörende Mahlzeit	😊 😐 ☹️

Ich kann schon auf Englisch fragen:

wie viel Uhr es ist	😊 😐 ☹️
welches Datum heute ist	😊 😐 ☹️
welcher Monat heute ist	😊 😐 ☹️
welcher Wochentag heute ist	😊 😐 ☹️

Ich kann schon auf Englisch lesen:

die Namen der Jahreszeiten und der Monate	😊 😐 ☹️
die Namen der Wochentage	😊 😐 ☹️
das Datum	😊 😐 ☹️
einen Stundenplan	😊 😐 ☹️
die Uhrzeit	😊 😐 ☹️

Ich bin mit mir sehr zufrieden. ◯

Ich finde, es war schon ganz gut. ◯

Ich hoffe, das wird noch besser. ◯

Transport

1. Do you know these means of transportation?

_____

_____ _____

_____ _____ _____ _____

_____ _____ _____

bike   car   lorry   motorbike   taxi   underground   bus   train   ferry   plane

2. Do you know the song: The Wheels on a Bus?
   To which means of transportation do these wheels belong?

These wheels belong to a   These wheels belong to a

 _____ .    _____ .

 _____    _____

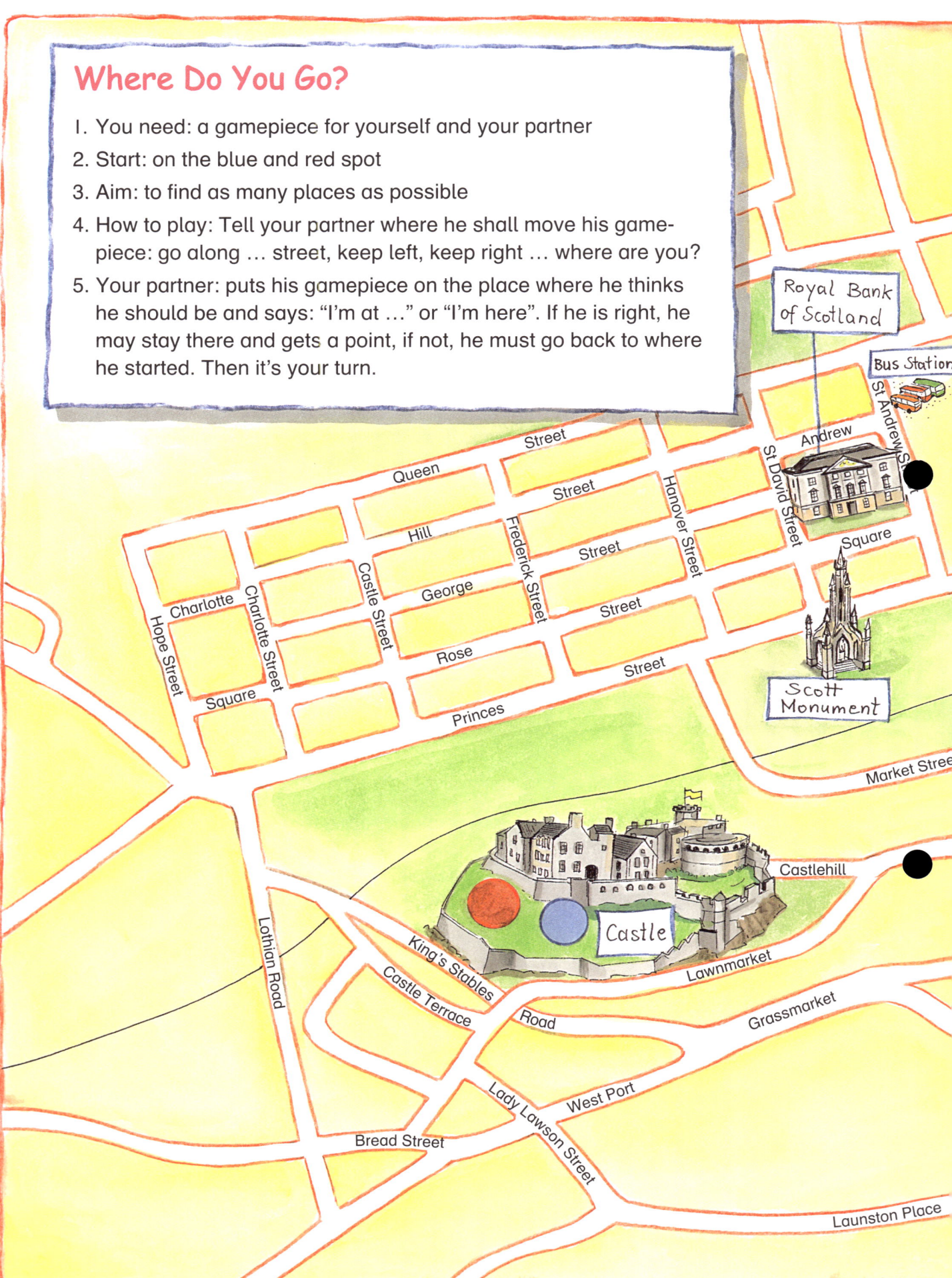

Where Do You Go?

1. You need: a gamepiece for yourself and your partner

2. Start: on the blue and red spot

3. Aim: to find as many places as possible

4. How to play: Tell your partner where he shall move his game-piece: go along … street, keep left, keep right … where are you?

5. Your partner: puts his gamepiece on the place where he thinks he should be and says: "I'm at …" or "I'm here". If he is right, he may stay there and gets a point, if not, he must go back to where he started. Then it's your turn.

Royal Bank of Scotland

Bus Station

St Andrews St

Andrew

St David Street

Square

Queen   Street

Street

Hill

Hanover Street

Frederick Street

Street

George

Castle Street

Charlotte

Charlotte Street

Street

Scott Monument

Hope Street

Rose

Street

Square

Street

Princes

Market Street

Castlehill

Castle

Lothian Road

King's Stables

Lawnmarket

Castle Terrace

Road

Grassmarket

Lady Lawson Street

West Port

Bread Street

Launston Place

British Money

tails

British Money

heads

Let's Go by Public Transport (p. 36)

If you want to buy a ticket, cut it out!

London (Pictures for p. 39)

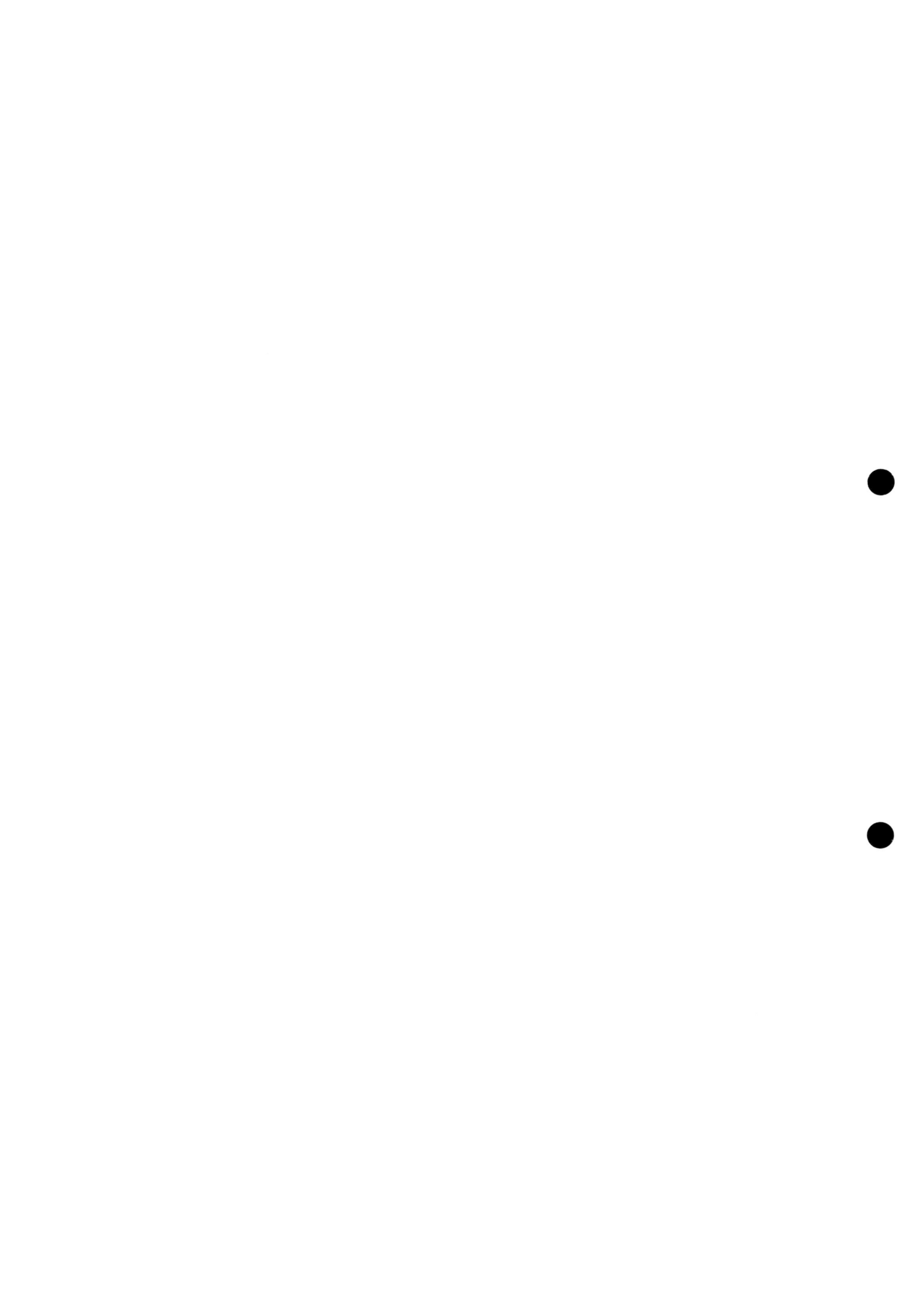

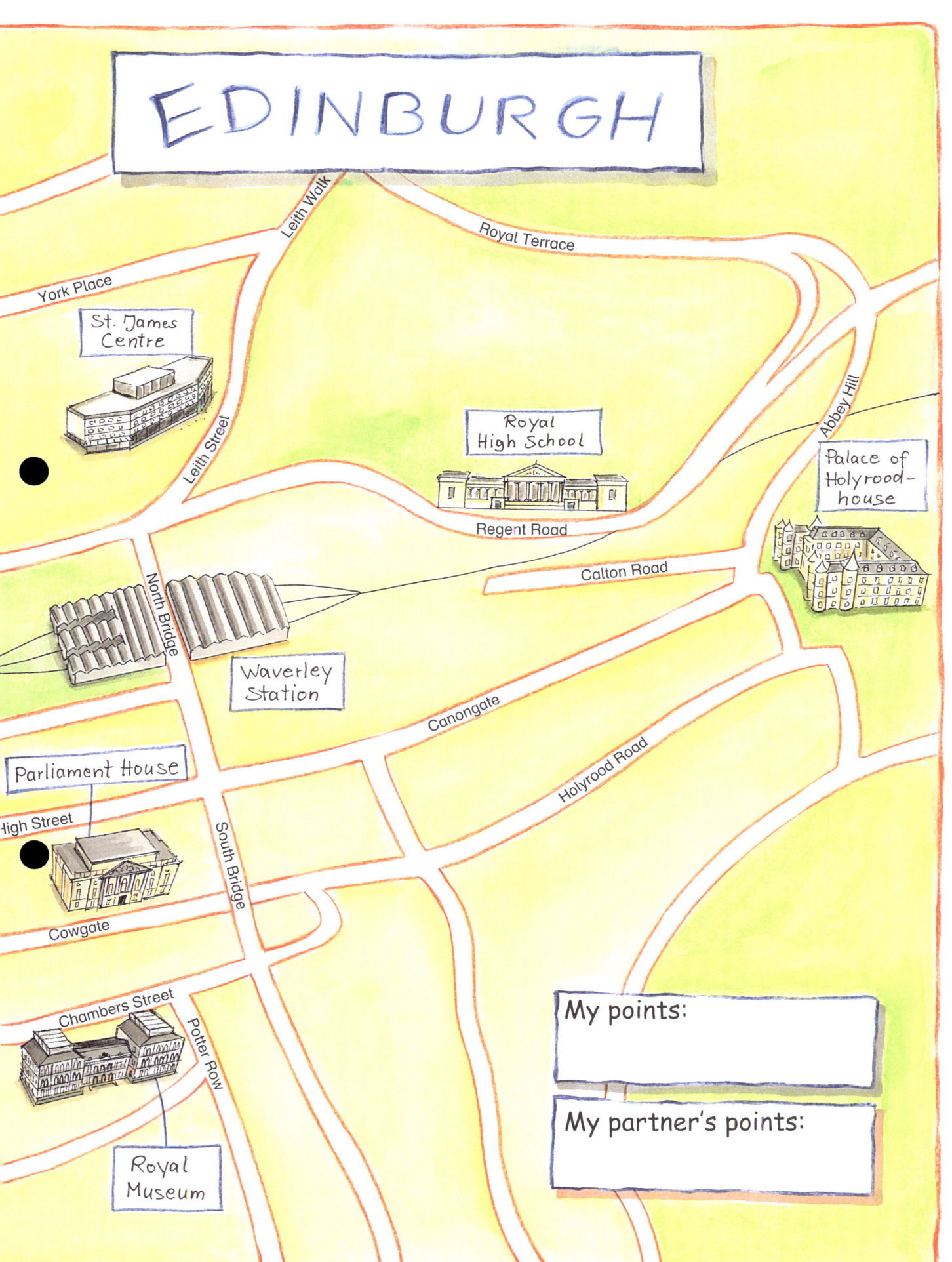

EDINBURGH

York Place

Leith Walk

Royal Terrace

St. James Centre

Leith Street

Royal High School

Abbey Hill

Palace of Holyrood-house

Regent Road

North Bridge

Calton Road

Waverley Station

Canongate

Parliament House

Holyrood Road

High Street

Cowgate

South Bridge

Chambers Street

Potter Row

Royal Museum

My points:

My partner's points:

Let's Go by Public Transport

1. Please read the dialogue with your friends.

Lisa and Peter want to travel to Britain.

Lisa:	I want to travel by plane. We will be in London in only two hours.
Peter:	But I'm afraid to fly. I want to take the bus.
Lisa:	You cannot travel by bus, Peter. The bus must go on a ferry then.
Peter:	Travelling by ferry is nice, too.
Lisa:	But we can also travel by train. There is a tunnel under the channel. So we do not need a ferry.
Peter:	That's good. Let's take the train.
Mum:	Oh children! We will travel by car.
Lisa and Peter:	But mum, there is a lot of water. Our car cannot swim!!!
Dad:	We can travel by train through the Eurotunnel with the car.
Lisa and Peter:	That's a good idea!

2. Let's buy a ticket!
   Write the correct names under the stations and the tickets.

plane ticket	harbour	train ticket	airport	bus ticket	bus stop
underground station		underground ticket		ferry ticket	train station

London

1. In London there are a lot of famous sights.
   Please fill in the names in the crossword puzzle.

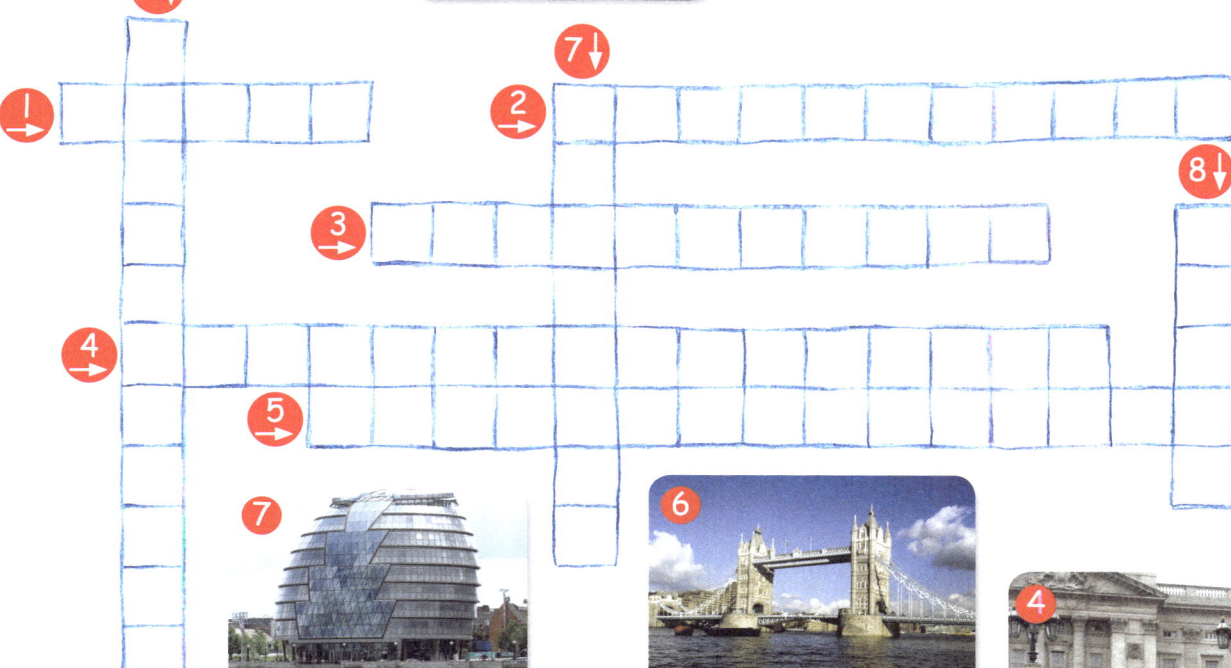

Across:
1. a London policeman
2. the Queen's treasure, worth a lot of money
3. it includes the Houses of Parliament and in the clocktower is Big Ben
4. this big house is the Queen's home in London
5. a famous place in the centre of London with a high column: around it is a fountain and the statues of four lions

Down:
6. a very famous sight over the river Thames with two big towers
7. a very modern building next to the river Thames
8. an old prison, one of the oldest houses in London

London – The Sights

1. Choose one of the next two pages.
   Can you find out the names of the sights?
   This one is easy!

This is the Queen's home in London. In front of the building there are many guards.

_____

She is the most famous woman in Britain. She lives in Buckingham Palace.

_____

It is an old prison. Guards called Beefeaters protect the crown jewels which you can see in this building.

_____

They are a treasure and belong to the Queen of England.

_____

It includes the houses of parliament, a big church and a clock tower. Every hour you can hear Big Ben.

_____

It is a bascule bridge with towers on both sides. It is the most famous sight in London.

_____

It is the nickname of a London city policeman.

_____

A very modern building near the Thames. The major of London works there.

_____

London – The Sights

This is difficult!

1. Cut out the pictures on page 33, glue them in and write the words.

In London people call a city policeman this name.

It includes the houses of parliament, a big abbey and a clocktower. Every hour you can hear Big Ben.

It is the most famous sight in London. It is a bascule bridge which opens for big ships. You can recognize it by the two towers.

It is an old prison. Guards called Beefeaters protect the crown jewels which you can see in this building.

This is the Queen's home in London. In front of the big palace there are many guards.

The major of London works there. It is a very modern building near the river Thames.

This valuable treasure you can see in the tower of London. It belongs to the Queen of England.

She lives in Buckingham Palace. She is the most famous woman in Britain.

London and Money

1. Please write the names of the coins and banknotes under the pictures:

_____   _____   _____

_____   _____   _____

_____   _____   _____

_____   _____   _____

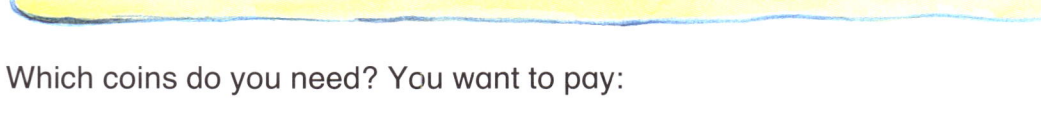

£2   £1   £50   £20   £5   £10   50p   10p   1 penny   20p   2p   5p

2. Which coins do you need? You want to pay:

£2.60   I need _____

£4.83   I need _____

97p   I need _____

Let's Go Shopping

1. Anna and David are in the city of London. Anna wants to buy some souvenirs for her parents and friends at home. Look what they find in a souvenir shop. Write the words under the matching prices.

£8.50

£4.89

£5.25

£2.95

£3.45

£4.28

85 p

£5.99

toy bus	postcard	football scarf	bag	baseball cap
	mug	T-shirt	toy letterbox	

2. Anna and David have got £15.

   Chose what they (**A+D**) buy and finish the dialogue with the shop assistant (**S.A.**):

A+D: Good _____ .

S.A.: Good afternoon. Can I _____ you?

A+D: We'd like _____ , please.

S.A.: That's _____ , please.

A+D: Here you _____ .

S.A.: _____ . Good _____ .

A+D: _____ .

help	afternoon	thank you	bye	Good bye
£_____	are	a _____	and a _____	

Let's Go Shopping

Peter and Lisa are in London, too. They also want to buy some souvenirs. They have got £15 each. Now they must calculate whether there is money left for a sandwich or a drink.

1. Read Peter's and Lisa's dialogue. Calculate the price.

Peter: I'd like a football scarf and a toy bus. I have 15 £.

Lisa: The scarf is £_____ and the toy bus is £_____.

£_____ + £_____ = £_____

Peter: £ 15 − £_____ = £_____

Lisa: Then you can still buy a drink. That is £_____.

2. Let Lisa buy something. Can you write the dialogue like in exercise 1.?

Lisa: _____

_____

Peter: _____

_____

Lisa: _____

_____

Peter: _____

_____

Portfolio: Public Transport, London and Money

I know means of transportation.
Name five of them:

_____

_____

I know the sights in London.
Write five of them:

_____

_____

I know the British money.
There are:

_____

I can calculate in English. Write the words under the calculations.

$$5 + 4 = 9 \qquad\qquad 7 - 4 = 3$$

_____   _____

That was 🙂 😐 🙁

Portfolio: Public Transport, London and Money

Ich kann schon auf Englisch verstehen:

	😊 😐 ☹️
wenn über Verkehrsmittel gesprochen wird	😊 😐 ☹️
wenn jemand sagt, ob ich ein- oder aussteigen soll	😊 😐 ☹️
wenn jemand sagt, in welche Richtung ich gehen soll	😊 😐 ☹️
wenn jemand über die Sehenswürdigkeiten Londons spricht	😊 😐 ☹️
wenn jemand eine Rechnung stellt	😊 😐 ☹️
wenn jemand über britisches Geld spricht	😊 😐 ☹️
wenn jemand mir eine Geldsumme sagt	😊 😐 ☹️
wie viel ich bezahlen muss	😊 😐 ☹️

Ich kann schon auf Englisch sagen:

wie die Verkehrsmittel heißen	😊 😐 ☹️
wie die Sehenswürdigkeiten Londons heißen	😊 😐 ☹️
was ich einkaufen will	😊 😐 ☹️
eine einfache Rechnung	😊 😐 ☹️
wie die Münzen des britischen Gelds heißen	😊 😐 ☹️
in welche Richtung jemand gehen soll	😊 😐 ☹️

Ich kann schon auf Englisch fragen:

wie viel etwas kostet	😊 😐 ☹️
wo eine Sehenswürdigkeit ist	😊 😐 ☹️
wohin ich gehen soll	😊 😐 ☹️
eine einfache Rechnung	😊 😐 ☹️

Ich kann schon auf Englisch lesen:

die Namen der Sehenswürdigkeiten Londons	😊 😐 ☹️
die Besonderheiten der Sehenswürdigkeiten	😊 😐 ☹️
die Namen der Verkehrsmittel	😊 😐 ☹️
ein Gespräch übers Einkaufen	😊 😐 ☹️
eine kleine Geschichte	😊 😐 ☹️
Preise auf Englisch	😊 😐 ☹️

 Ich bin mit mir sehr zufrieden. ⭕

 Ich finde, es war schon ganz gut. ⭕

 Ich hoffe, das wird noch besser. ⭕

The Creature with no Name – The Words

1. Write the correct numbers next to the pictures.

(1) big head
(2) purple eyes
(3) bright yellow eyebrows
(4) small hands

(5) small feet
(6) left leg shorter than the right one
(7) soft red fur

2. Can you write the correct phrases next to the matching pictures?

The creature has …

The Creature with no Name

Deep in the dark woods lives a horrible looking creature with no name. In his head which is too big there are purple eyes with bright yellow eyebrows. His hands and feet are too small. Because his left leg is shorter than the right one the creature limps when it is walking. The only nice thing is his soft fur. But the fur is not lovely brown, it is bright red. Everybody in the woods knows the ugly creature with no name. And everybody is frightened. "The creature with no name eats all other animals," they say. So the creature with no name has no friends and is very sad.

But one day he meets a little mouse. He thinks that the mouse will run away. But the mouse stands there and looks at him. "Who are you? What's your name?" the little mouse asks. "I don't have a name," he says. "No name? Shall I give you a name?" The creature thinks about it. Then he says: "That's a good idea." "Ok, let me think… Can you help me, children?" the mouse asks.

1. Can **you** give him a name? Please write it in the gaps.

_____ has a name now. He is very happy. The next day he goes

through the woods again. "Hello _____ ," says the snake.

"Hello _____ ," says the fox and "hello _____ ,"
says the owl. Nobody is frightened any more. "Why are you not frightened?"

_____ asks. "Because now we know you and you've got a lovely
name," the animals answer.

2. Mark ☒ the correct answer.

Where does the creature live?
- ☐ in a dark house
- ☐ in the dark woods

Why does he have to limp?
- ☐ because he cannot walk
- ☐ because one leg is too short

Does the mouse run away?
- ☐ No, she was not frightened.
- ☐ Yes, but she asked for his name.

How does she help the poor creature?
- ☐ She knows that he needs a name and asks the children for help.
- ☐ She does not know what to do and asks the children for help.

3. What did the creature look like? Describe!

_____

_____

_____

The Creature with no Name

1. Here you can see two persons.
   You shall create two very ugly creatures
   like the creature with no name:

Draw a big head.	–	Draw a very small head.
Draw two big green eyes.	–	Draw one big eye in the middle of the face.
Draw two thick arms.	–	Draw two thin arms.
Draw a big body.	–	Draw a thin body.
Draw two short thick legs.	–	Draw two long thin legs.
…	–	…

   Colour in!

2. Talk to your partner about your funny creatures.

Welcome to Scotland!

1. Anna and Michael come from Scotland.
   Here you can see the Scottish flag.
   Colour it in!

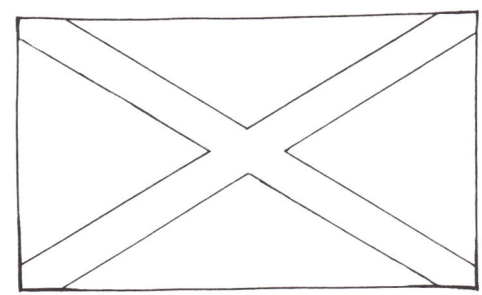

2. Can you write down what you can see in these pictures?

_____ _____ _____ _____

_____ _____ _____ _____

_____

> bagpipes   curling   golf   Edinburgh Castle   Stirling Castle
> Eilean Donan Castle   Loch Ness   Nessie

3. Listen to the Scottish National Anthem. Try to read while you are singing!

1./4.	2.	3.
O Flower of Scotland	The Hills are bare now,	Those days are past now,
When will we see	And Autumn leaves	And in the past
Your like again,	Lie thick and still,	They must remain,
That fought and died for,	O'er land that is lost now,	But we can still rise now,
Your wee bit hill and glen,	Which those so dearly held,	And be the nation again,
And stood against him,	That stood against him,	That stood against him,
Proud Edward's army,	Proud Edward's army,	Proud Edward's army,
And sent him homeward,	And sent him homeward,	And sent him homeward,
Tae think again.	Tae think again.	Tae think again.

Scotland

Rodney the Sheep

Rodney lives in the Scottish Highlands. He is not the only sheep there. He has 57 brothers and 128 sisters.
But Rodney does not want to stay in the Highlands. One day he leaves the meadow and goes to a big lake.

There he can see something very big in the lake.
Hello. I'm Rodney the sheep. Who are you?
I'm Nessie and I live here in Loch Ness.
What is a loch? Loch is the Scottish word for lake. I want to see Scotland.
Where shall I go?
Go to Edinburgh. Edinburgh is the capital of Scotland.

So Rodney goes to Edinburgh. It is a very big city with a big castle. He sees a sheep in a meadow.
Hello. I'm Rodney the sheep. Who are you?
I'm Donna.
Edinburgh is so big. Is it the biggest city in Scotland?

No, Glasgow is bigger. It is the biggest city.
How do I get to Glasgow?
You must go through the glen and over the hills.
What is a glen?
A glen is a valley between mountains.

So Rodney goes over the hills and through the glen. There he meets a funny animal. It looks like a cow with very long fur.
Hello. I'm Rodney the sheep. Who are you?
I'm Henry the Highland cow.

Why do the men wear skirts in Scotland?
They don't wear skirts. They wear kilts.
Ok. And what does that white cross on the blue flag mean?

It is the Scottish flag. You don't know a lot about Scotland, Rodney. Trooooooooo! Rodney gets a fright.
What is this?
These are bagpipes. I think you better go home and read a book about Scotland.

Rodney is very tired. So he goes home and stays in the meadow with his 57 brothers and 128 sisters.
And he tells them a lot about Edinburgh, kilts, bagpipes and big cities.

What Do You Know about Scotland?

Play with a partner.
You need: a gamepiece each and a dice. Throw the dice. The one with the highest roll of the dice starts. Put your gamepieces on "START". You move your gamepiece according to the points on the dice anywhere on the gameboard. On some spaces you must find an answer. The words in the box will help you.

If you can find the answer, you may colour in the white spot. If you cannot you do not do anything. The "Nessies" are your jokers. When you get there just colour the spot. Winner is the one who could colour in the most white spots.

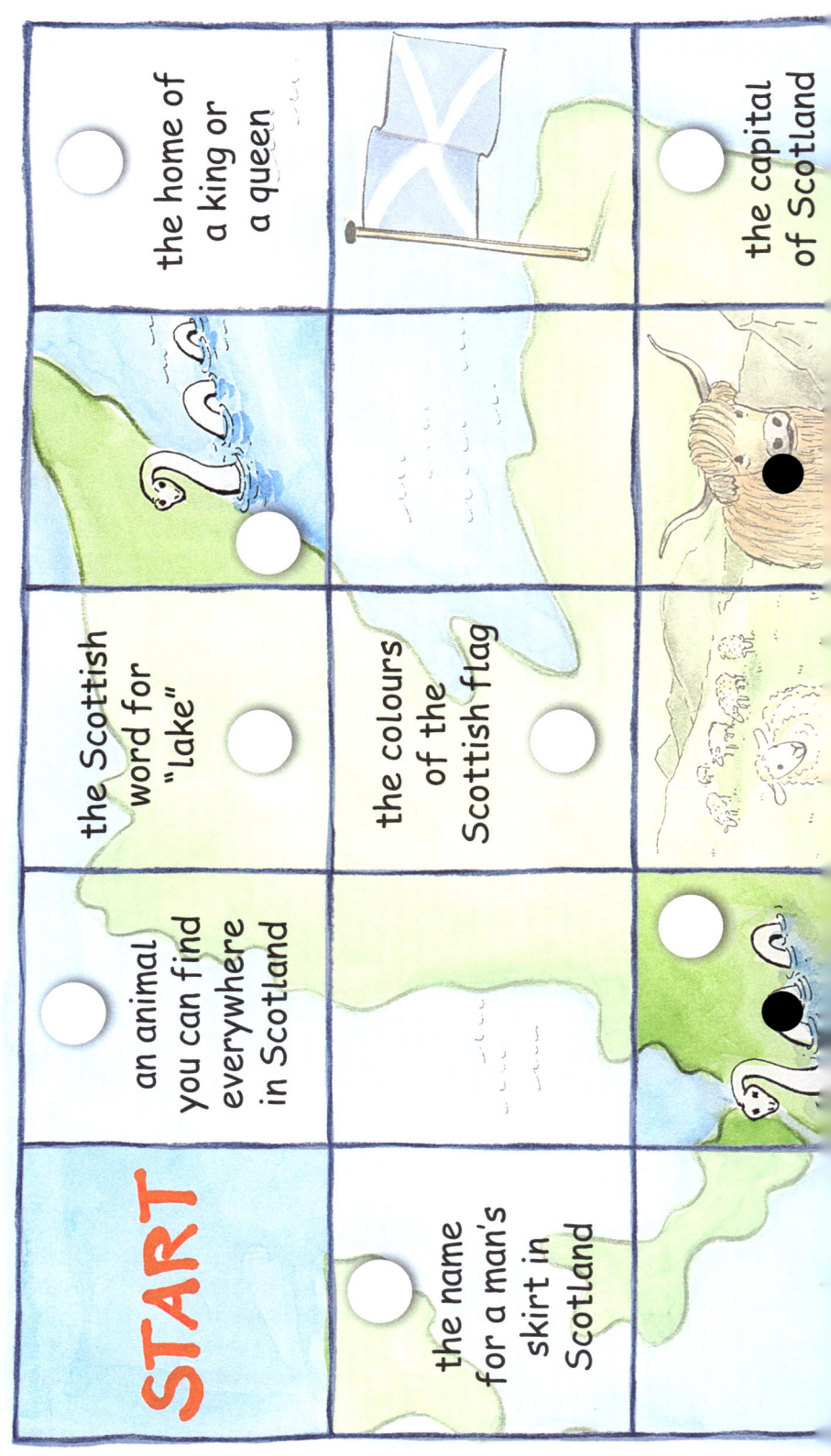

the home of
a king or
a queen

the capital
of Scotland

the Scottish
word for
"lake"

the colours
of the
Scottish flag

an animal
you can find
everywhere
in Scotland

START

the name
for a man's
skirt in
Scotland

	a famous Scottish instrument	
I am a big animal that lives in Scotland. I am brown and have long fur.		the biggest city in Scotland
	the Scottish word for "valley"	Who lives in Loch Ness?
the region in Scotland where Rodney comes from	the field where a sheep lives	

sheep   loch   Nessie   Highland cow   castle

glen   Edinburgh   meadow   blue and white   Inverness

Glasgow   bagpipes   kilt

Sport in Scotland

What do you know about sport?

1. Read the little texts. Write the correct letter in the little spots above:

A This sport was invented in Scotland. You have to walk long distances to play it. You need clubs and balls. The playing areas are called greens, tees and fairways.

B This sport was invented in Scotland, too. Outdoor you can only play it in winter. But there are indoor halls in the meantime. You play in a team of four players and you need stones to play it. The playing area is called a sheet.

C This sport was not originally invented in Scotland, but it is one of the most famous sports in Scotland. You play it in a team. And you need a ball shaped like an egg for it. The playing area is called a pitch.

D This is the most famous sport not only in Scotland. You play it on a pitch, too. In every team there are eleven players. On both sides of the pitch there is a goal.

2. Can you fill in the missing words?

1. Football is a very famous _____ . Many boys and girls in Germany

   love to _____ it, too. In every team there are _____ players. You

   must kick a ball into a _____ . The team who scores the most goals wins.

2. Rugby is a very rough _____ . You are allowed to push the other players

   to get the _____ . The ball looks a bit like an _____ . In one team

   there are fifteen or thirteen _____ .

3. Curling was invented in _____ . In one team are _____

   players. You play with _____ .

4. Golf is played on _____ , _____ and _____ .

   You must try and putt the ball with a _____ into the hole.

Sport

There are many sports.

1. Do you know them all? Write the names under the pictures.

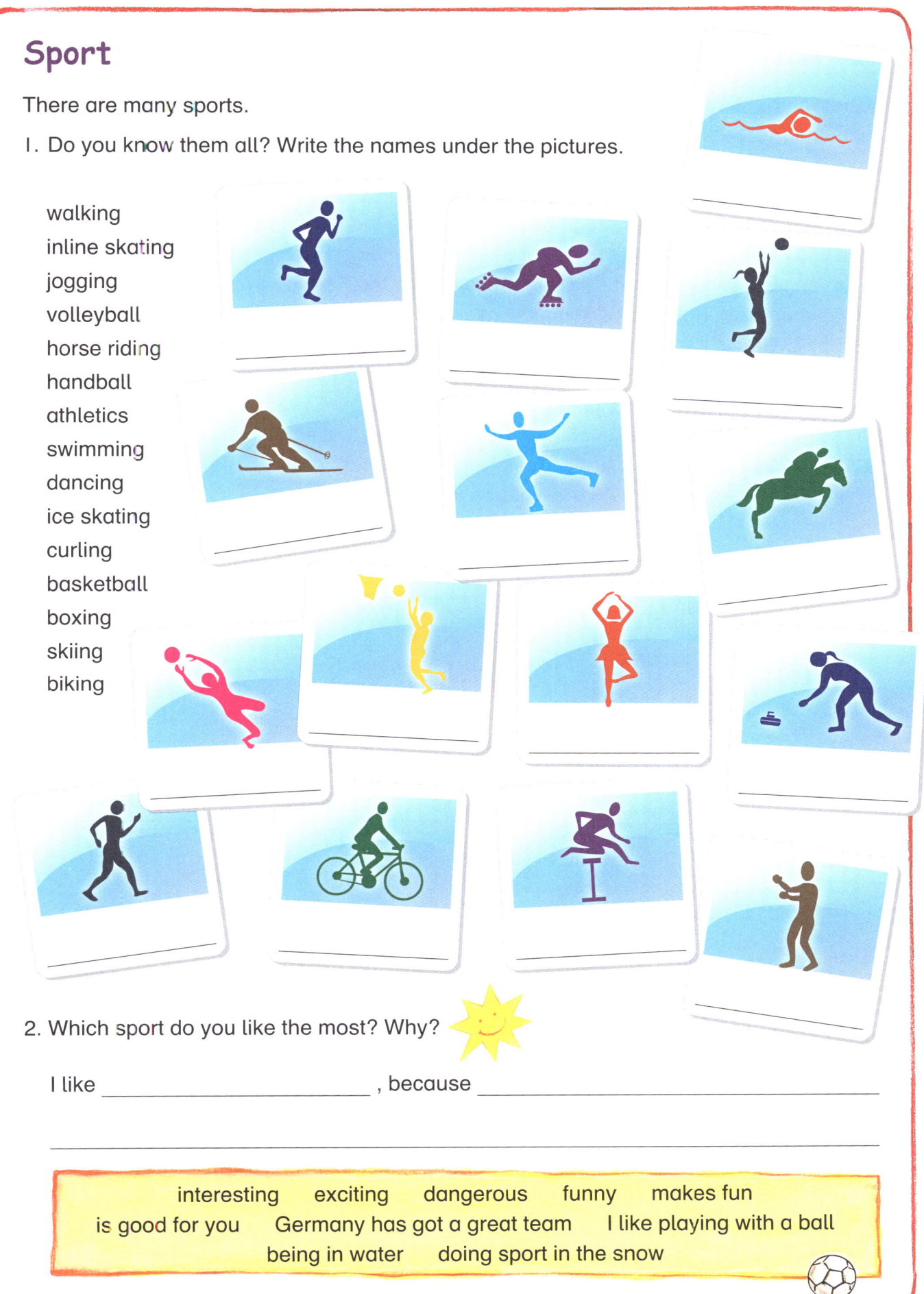

walking
inline skating
jogging
volleyball
horse riding
handball
athletics
swimming
dancing
ice skating
curling
basketball
boxing
skiing
biking

2. Which sport do you like the most? Why?

I like _____ , because _____

_____

| interesting   exciting   dangerous   funny   makes fun |
| is good for you   Germany has got a great team   I like playing with a ball |
| being in water   doing sport in the snow |

My Favourite Sports

What is your favourite sport?
Lisa and Peter visit Anna and Michael in Edinburgh.
The Scottish children tell the German boy and girl that football
is very important in Scotland.
Peter says: "In Germany football is very important, too".
"But you need many people to play it. I love horseriding," Lisa says.
"But you need a horse for it. Riding my bike is fun, too," Anna says.
"My favourite sport is rugby," Michael says.
"Rugby? What is that?" the German children ask.
"Rugby was not invented in Scotland. But like Scotsmen it is very tough. You've got to be a real man," Michael explains.
"A real man?" Anna starts laughing. "And what about last time? He fell off his bike and skinned his knee. Then he started crying like a little girl."
Michael's cheeks turn red. All the children laugh.

1. Can you answer these questions? (Try and use full sentences!)

Where are Lisa and Peter from? _____

What is Peter's favourite sport? _____

What is Lisa's favourite sport? _____

What is Anna's favourite sport? _____

What is Michael's favourite sport? _____

Why is football Peter's favourite sport? Because _____

Why does Lisa not like football? _____

Why does Anna like riding a bike? _____

Why does Michael like rugby? _____

Why do the children laugh? _____

_____

_____

The Maze

1. Do you know them all? Write the names under the pictures.

What is a knight without a **sword**? _____

He has to pick up the sword first.

Now he has got the sword. _____

But he is not complete yet.

He needs his **shield**.

And a knight needs a **horse**, too.

Take him to his horse. _____

Then he meets a second **knight**.

He wants the princess, too.

He has to fight with him.

And he is stronger. _____

Under a tree he finds a **key**.

He does not know whether he will need it.

But he puts it in his pocket.

In front of a cave there is a **dragon**. _____

He fights the dragon and wins.

Then he reaches the **castle's draw bridge**.

He rides over the bridge.

In front of the door there is a gate.

The **gate** is locked. _____

But with the key he can open it.

In the castle yard there are the **king and the queen**.

They say: "If you can win against the ghost

you will get the princess and the treasure."

So the knight must go to the **tower**.

Under the tower there is a **dungeon**.

It is dark and scary. _____

In the dungeon there is the **ghost**.

But he is a nice ghost and he promises to go to another castle.

In the dungeon there is a **ring**.

The knight takes the ring. _____

Then he goes to the **princess**.

The princess sits on the **treasure box**.

He gives the ring to the princess and

they become husband and wife.

And the knight gets the **crown**. _____

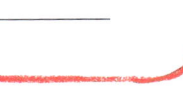

A Maze - Help the Knight!

1. Can you help the knight to find his way to the princess? Look at page 55 for help!

Kings and Queens and Castles

Let's Go on a Castle Tour!

Lisa and Peter are still at Anna's and Michael's home in Edinburgh.

One day Michael asks: "Do you like castles?"

"Castles and palaces are boring," Peter says.

"So you don't like playing knight at all?" Anna asks.

"Of course I do." Peter answers.

"Let's go on a castle tour then," the two Scottish children say.

Do you want to go with them? Let's go!

Now we are in England. Here is Leeds Castle. It is a water palace in the south of England. It is 1200 years old and we can find the only museum in the world for dog's collars. We can stay here for a holiday.

Let's start in Edinburgh. Edinburgh Castle is about 700 years old. We can see a very big canon that still works: It is called the one o'clock gun and every day at 1 o'clock you can hear it everywhere in the city. A real canon is great!

In the west of Scotland is one of the most beautiful water castles in Scotland. It is called Eilean Donan Castle. And it is about 800 years old. In the castle you can see everything about life in the 13th century.

Not far from Edinburgh is Stirling. There is Stirling Castle. It really looks like a very old castle with princesses and knights. Stirling Castle is 900 years old. Most of the Scottish kings lived here. And some films were taken here.

Dover Castle is about 1000 years old and it has a lighthouse. From high up there we can look down to the sea, the channel. You see the castle if you cross the channel by ferry.

Let's go back to Great Britain. We go to Wales. There is a big castle, too. It is called Harlech Castle. And it is also

800 years old. It is only a ruin, but there we can play hide and seek with knights and kings. A wonderful place to play.

Let's go to Ireland now. In the south of Ireland there is Blackrock Castle. "There is a game in Germany called Blackrock Castle," Peter says. In the castle you can see lots of stars because it is a centre of astronomy.

1. At home again mum asks a lot of questions. Can you help the children to answer them?

Did you see a water castle?

☐ a) Yes, it is called _____.
☐ b) No, there was no water castle.
☐ c) Yes, all of them were water castles.

What's the name of the Irish castle?

☐ a) Eilean Donan Castle
☐ b) Dover Castle
☐ c) Blackrock Castle

Could you see a real canon that is still working?

☐ a) No, that is too dangerous.
☐ b) All castles have working canons.
☐ c) Yes, it was in _____.

Where could you play knight and king?

☐ a) It was very good at _____.
☐ b) No, we were not allowed to play anywhere.
☐ c) Yes, we just played it everywhere.

What are the names of the Scottish castles?

☐ a) Blackrock Castle, Edinburgh Castle,
    Eilean Donan Castle
☐ b) Dover Castle, Stirling Castle, Edinburgh Castle
☐ c) Edinburgh Castle, Stirling Castle,
    Eilean Donan Castle

Can you name the English castles?

_____

_____

Where is Harlech Castle?

☐ a) in Wales
☐ b) in Scotland
☐ c) in England

The Grand Old Duke of York

1. Listen to the song while you are reading. Then fill in the missing words.

The Grand Old Duke of York

The grand old Duke of Y __ __ __ ,

He had ten thousand m __ __ ,

He marched them up to the t __ __ of the hill.

And he marched them d __ __ __ again.

And when they were u __ they were up,

And when t __ __ __ were down they were down.

And when they were o __ __ __ half-way up.

They w __ __ __ neither up nor down.

up	were
men	York
only	down
top	they

2. Let's dance:

The grand old Duke of York.

Stand opposite your partner. Walk in place. Put your hand at your head like a soldier.

He had ten thousand men.

Stretch your arms to the front and shake your ten fingers.

He marched them up to the top of the hill.

Bend your knees, raise to the front and hold your arms over your head.

And he marched them down again.

Go back down, bend your knees.

And when they were up they were up.

Stretch your arms over your head and jump.

And when they were down they were down.

Bend your knees.

And when they were only half-way up.

Stand up but only half-way.

They were neither up nor down.

Stretch your arms over your head, jump once, then bend your knees.

Sleeping Beauty

1. Write the blue text of the song under the matching pictures.

There Was a Princess Long Ago
– Dornröschen war ein schönes Kind –

There was a princess long ago,
Long ago, long ago;
There was a princess long ago,
Long, long ago.

And she lived in a big high tower,
A big high tower, a big high tower;
And she lived in a big high tower,
Long, long ago.

A wicked fairy cast a spell,
Cast a spell, cast a spell;
A wicked fairy cast a spell,
Long, long ago.

The princess slept for a hundred years,
A hundred years, a hundred years;
The princess slept for a hundred years,
Long, long ago.

A great big forest grew around,
Grew around, grew around;
A great big forest grew around,
Long, long ago.

A handsome prince came riding by,
Riding by, riding by;
A handsome prince came riding by,
Long, long ago.

He chopped the trees down with his sword,
With his sword, with his sword;
He chopped the trees down with his sword,
Long, long ago.

He woke the princess with a kiss,
With a kiss, with a kiss;
He woke the princess with a kiss,
Long, long ago.

So everybody's happy now,
Happy now, happy now;
So everybody's happy now,
Happy now.

What a Night!

1. Please read the little book up to page 9. Can you tick ✓ the correct answers?

                                                                    right wrong
   a) The Olsons live in a modern house.   ☐   ☐
   b) Stella the cat and Ginnie the parrot are old.   ☐   ☐
   c) Ginnie sleeps in its cage.   ☐   ☐
   d) Stella sleeps under the sofa.   ☐   ☐
   e) Osko and his dad are two rats.   ☐   ☐
   f) Mr and Mrs Olson like the mice.   ☐   ☐
   g) Osko thinks life at the Olsons' is boring.   ☐   ☐
   h) His dad thinks that it is dangerous outside the house.   ☐   ☐

2. Please read up to page 19. Can you answer these questions?

   a) Osko meets other animals. Which ones? _____

   b) Osko flies from the cat. Where did he go?
      ☐ into an old watering can
      ☐ into an old bucket
      ☐ into a mouse hole

   c) Osko hears a noise above him. It sounds like a flying bird. What is it?
      ☐ Ginnie
      ☐ a budgie
      ☐ an owl

   d) A bat talks to Osko. He says:
      ☐ "I want to eat you."
      ☐ "Cats and owls can't be your friends."
      ☐ "Life sometimes is wonderful."

3. Please read the rest of the book. Can you answer these questions, too?
   a) What does Osko's dad ask him?

   _____

   b) Why can Osko not answer any more?

   _____

4. There are many things in the Olson's food store. Cross out ✕✕✕ the things you cannot find there:

   | milk | bread | butter | biscuits | sandwiches | cake |
   | pizza | cheese | jam | honey | sugar | chocolate |

What a night – Time for stories, www.mildenberger-verlag.de/time-for-stories

Portfolio: Scotland, Sports, Castles

I know a lot of English words and sentences.

What do you think: How many words do you know in English?

I think I know _____ words and _____ sentences.

I can ask many things in English.

What do you think: How many things can you ask in English?

I think I can ask _____ things.

I know Great Britain. Which countries are in Great Britain? _____

_____

These are my favourite English words:

_____

_____

_____

That was 😊 😐 ☹

Hello Rodney!

Portfolio: Scotland, Sports, Castles

Ich kann schon auf Englisch verstehen:

	😊 😐 ☹️
wenn über Schottland gesprochen wird	😊 😐 ☹️
wenn jemand ein Märchen über Könige und Ritter erzählt	😊 😐 ☹️
auch längere englische Bilderbücher	😊 😐 ☹️
Einzelheiten aus Büchern und Geschichten	😊 😐 ☹️
wenn jemand von Sehenswürdigkeiten und Burgen spricht	😊 😐 ☹️
wenn jemand nach Wörtern und Sätzen fragt	😊 😐 ☹️
wenn jemand begründet, warum er etwas mag	😊 😐 ☹️
wenn jemand begründet, warum er etwas nicht mag	😊 😐 ☹️

Ich kann schon auf Englisch sagen:

	😊 😐 ☹️
einige Sehenswürdigkeiten und Burgen	😊 😐 ☹️
einige Dinge aus längeren englischen Bilderbüchern	😊 😐 ☹️
was mir am besten gefällt und warum	😊 😐 ☹️
das Wichtigste über eine Sportart	😊 😐 ☹️
welche Sportart ich gerne mache	😊 😐 ☹️

Ich kann schon auf Englisch fragen:

	😊 😐 ☹️
was jemand am besten gefällt und warum	😊 😐 ☹️
was jemandes Lieblingssportart ist	😊 😐 ☹️
wie alt eine Burg ist	😊 😐 ☹️
wo eine Sehenswürdigkeit ist	😊 😐 ☹️

Ich kann schon auf Englisch lesen:

	😊 😐 ☹️
die Namen der Sehenswürdigkeiten in Schottland	😊 😐 ☹️
die Namen einiger Burgen auf den Britischen Inseln	😊 😐 ☹️
schwierige Wörter aus längeren Bilderbüchern	😊 😐 ☹️
Informationen zu Bildern	😊 😐 ☹️
kleine Geschichten auf Englisch	😊 😐 ☹️

Ich bin mit mir sehr zufrieden. ◯

Ich finde, es war schon ganz gut. ◯

Ich hoffe, das wird noch besser. ◯